Library Resources

What Would You Do with a
Thesaurus?

Susan Kralovansky

Consulting Editor, Diane Craig, M.A./Reading Specialist

A Division of ABDO

ABDO
Publishing Company

visit us at www.abdopublishing.com

Published by ABDO Publishing Company, a division of ABDO, P.O. Box 398166, Minneapolis, Minnesota 55439. Copyright © 2013 by Abdo Consulting Group, Inc. International copyrights reserved in all countries. No part of this book may be reproduced in any form without written permission from the publisher. Super SandCastle™ is a trademark and logo of ABDO Publishing Company.

Printed in the United States of America, North Mankato, Minnesota
102012
012013

♻ PRINTED ON RECYCLED PAPER

Editor: Liz Salzmann
Content Developer: Nancy Tuminelly
Cover and Interior Design and Production: Kelly Doudna, Mighty Media, Inc.
Photo Credits: Shutterstock, Thinkstock

Library of Congress Cataloging-in-Publication Data

Kralovansky, Susan.
  What would you do with a thesaurus? / Susan Kralovansky.
    p. cm. -- (Library resources)
  ISBN 978-1-61783-605-3
  1. English language--Synonyms and antonyms--Juvenile literature. 2. Thesauri--Juvenile literature. I. Title.
  423--dc15

                             2012946803

Super SandCastle™ books are created by a team of professional educators, reading specialists, and content developers around five essential components—phonemic awareness, phonics, vocabulary, text comprehension, and fluency—to assist young readers as they develop reading skills and strategies and increase their general knowledge. All books are written, reviewed, and leveled for guided reading, early reading intervention, and Accelerated Reader® programs for use in shared, guided, and independent reading and writing activities to support a balanced approach to literacy instruction.

Contents

What would you do if you had a thesaurus?

If you had a thesaurus, you could always find the right word.
The right word for what?
The right word for anything!

The Thesaurus

A thesaurus gives you choices for words. It lists other words that mean the same thing. It also lists words that mean the opposite.

thesaurus
how many words do you know?

word games | word of the day | new words

search thesaurus...

Good *(adjective)*

Synonyms 6
fine, pleasant, excellent, great, decent, correct,

You can find words to use in a letter or a story.

You can look up words in a book or online.

Letters are more interesting
if you use different words.
A thesaurus can help.

Dear Mom and Dad,

Camp is good. The counselors
are good. The food is not
good. Please send cookies.

Love, Jake

good = fine

good, *adjective* fine, pleasant, excellent, great, decent, correct, proper, wonderful, dear, special. ANTONYMS awful, bad, wicked, evil, unpleasant.

not good = awful

good = great

Dear Mom and Dad,

Camp is fine. The counselors are great. The food is awful. Please send cookies.

Love, Jake

The word you look up is called the entry word.

 The largest thesaurus has 920,000 entry words.

Dear Mom and Dad,

Camp is good. The counselors are good. The food is not good. Please send cookies.

Love, Jake

entry word

good, *adjective* fine, pleasant, excellent, great, decent, correct, proper, wonderful, dear, special. ANTONYMS **awful**, bad, wicked, evil, unpleasant.

The entry words are in alphabetical order. The top of each page has two guide words. They are the first and last entry words on the page.

Let's say the guide words are *paddle* and *panda*. The word *pail* will be on that page. But the word *parrot* will not be.

paddle **panda**

paddle
page
pagoda
pail
painful
paint
pajamas

pal
palace
pale
palm
pamper
pan
panda

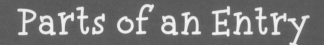
A thesaurus lists synonyms and antonyms for each entry word.

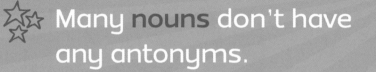

Many **nouns** don't have any antonyms.

14

Entry Word	Part of Speech	Synonyms	Antonyms
calm	*adjective*	cool, quiet, gentle, mild, still, tranquil, relaxed, serene, hushed, low-key	excited, mad, upset
little	*adjective*	small, tiny, wee, slight, teeny, mini, miniature, dinky, puny, itty-bitty	huge, big, large
house	*noun*	home, dwelling, lodging, cottage, mansion, shanty, hut, shack	—
run	*verb*	jog, dart, trip, race, hurry, fly, rush, bound, speed	walk, crawl, creep

Synonyms are words that have the same meaning.

Some synonyms for *horse* are *steed*, *mount*, and *nag*.

horse, *noun*
equine, stallion, mare, gelding, colt, filly, steed, mount, pony, nag, charger, bronco.

horse

nag

steed

17

mount

Antonyms are words
with opposite meanings.

Antonyms
are listed after
the synonyms.
Tiny is an antonym
for *large*.

18

large, *adjective* **big, great, huge, giant, tall, vast, bulky, hefty, solid, sturdy, fat, plump, ample, wide, broad. ANTONYMS small, little, tiny, thin, meager, trivial.**

The cat was large but the mouse was tiny!

Many synonyms can be used in place of each other.

funny, *adjective* humorous, witty, comic, silly, wacky, amusing, hilarious, odd, weird, strange. ANTONYMS serious, sad, unamusing, unfunny, dramatic.

funny

humorous

hilarious

The school play was funny.

The school play was humorous.

The school play was hilarious.

But some synonyms can't always be used for each other.

Ian's hands are dirty!

Ian's hands are filthy!

Ian's hands are polluted!

Ian's hands are polluted? That doesn't sound right.

dirty

filthy

dirty, *adjective* filthy, grimy, muddy, grubby, slimy, unclean, stained, gross, soiled, unwashed, polluted. ANTONYMS clean, pure, washed, spotless, neat, spic-and-span.

23

polluted

Why Use a Thesaurus?

Why
do we need
a thesaurus?
Why not just use
a dictionary?

A dictionary tells you what a word means. But what if you want other ways to say the same thing? That's what a thesaurus is for.

 The word *thesaurus* means *treasure* in Latin.

Use a thesaurus to make your sentences more interesting.

dark, *adjective* inky, dingy, dusky, gloomy, shady, dim, unlit.

cloudy, *adjective* hazy, overcast, misty, foggy, blurred, murky, milky.

It was a ~~dark~~ gloomy, ~~cloudy~~ foggy night.

The ~~dogs~~ pooches wore ~~funny~~ goofy costumes.

Use a thesaurus to make your sentences more exciting.

dog, *noun* hound, pup, cur, mongrel, whelp, pooch, mutt.

funny, *adjective* amusing, humorous, jolly, goofy, clever, odd, strange, weird.

With a thesaurus you'll always find the right word!

hat, *noun* cap, derby, bowler, turban, Stetson, helmet, tam, sombrero, chullo, top hat, fedora, bonnet, cloche, lid, headdress, headgear.

bowler

chullo

cloche

sombrero

helmet

cap

top hat

31

Glossary

alphabetical – arranged in the order of the letters of the alphabet.

counselor – a person who gives advice to others.

Latin – the language of ancient Rome.

noun – a word that is a person, place, or thing. *Father*, *barn*, and *kite* are all nouns.